SLAVERY

IN

THE UNITED STATES:

ITS

EVILS, ALLEVIATIONS, AND REMEDIES.

REPRINTED FROM THE NORTH AMERICAN REVIEW, OCT. 1851.

BOSTON:
CHARLES C. LITTLE AND JAMES BROWN.
1851.

Whoever reads these remarks will see that the subject under discussion is treated solely as a great social question; that the object has been to state some of the more material facts, which must necessarily control action in regard to it, and to suggest some practicable method of diminishing the evils of slavery, or of removing it altogether. Whether wisely or unwisely, all reference to its bearings on the politics of the day has been carefully avoided. Amidst all the changes of parties, slavery remains among us, and there seems but slight reason to anticipate any great improvement in the condition of the colored race in this country, through political action. At any rate, it cannot be undesirable to keep in view any other modes of action which are within our power; while the expression of the hope may be permitted, that a discussion of the subject in a manner so aside from its party relations may do something to promote a better and more friendly understanding between those whom the complex questions of the time have brought into temporary opposition and conflict. In reprinting the article, a few verbal alterations have been made, but they are of too little importance to require any special notice.

SLAVERY IN THE UNITED STATES.*

It would be very surprising if the institution of Slavery were not the occasion of ceaseless discussion and agitation in the United States. It is a matter of vital interest to the South, and, indirectly, of scarcely less moment to the North. Its existence must of necessity be taken into the account as a main element in determining the policy of the General Government; political parties gravitate around it as if it were a fixed magnetic centre; it exerts a controlling influence over the industrial pursuits and relations of the country; and, what is of not less importance, creates around itself a peculiar social state and classes of interests which have been, and are likely to be, the occasion of perpetual irritation between the North and South.

It is a subject, which, above all others debated among us, ought to be treated with calmness and candor; and, happily, there seems to be prevailing a fairer and more conciliatory spirit, and a growing disposition to transfer its discussion from the tribunal of the passions to that of the judgment. The temporary lull of political excitement furnishes a fitting opportunity for presenting some of those considerations respecting the more general aspects of slavery which are essential to the formation of just conclusions, but which, in seasons of party strife, are apt to be neglected. How far and how fast is the institution of slavery susceptible of change and amelioration — what are the prospects of its being removed — and what can be done to promote its removal; —

---

* 1. *Jamaica in 1850: or the Effects of Sixteen Years of Freedom on a Slave Colony.* By John Bigelow. Magnas inter opes inops: Horace. New York and London: George P. Putman. 1851. 16mo. pp. 214.

2. *First Annual Report of the Trustees of Donations for Education in Liberia.* Presented at the Annual Meeting, January 15, 1851. Boston: T. R. Marvin. 1851.

3. *Abstract of the Seventh Census: Aggregate, by States, of the White, Free Colored, and Slave Population of the United States, in 1850.* Published in the National Intelligencer. Washington.

these are the great practical questions which present themselves to most minds. We propose to consider them, partly on account of their intrinsic interest, but with a particular reference to their bearing on the subject of African colonization.

It is conceded on all hands, that the right to legislate in regard to slavery belongs exclusively to the individual States in which that institution exists. Each State has the right to abolish slavery within its own borders, and no other State is permitted to interfere with its action. The General Government may, at most, admit it into, or exclude it from, the Territories of the Union, though, even in regard to the right of exercising this power, there is not universal agreement. But its authority certainly ceases when the Territories become States. This single consideration, without reference to any thing else, shows that the direct power, both of the General Government and of the Free States over slavery, is confined within very narrow limits. Instead of the several States deriving from the Union authority to interfere with one another's domestic institutions, the organic law by which they are united excludes them from such interference, and at the same time relieves them from a corresponding responsibility.

There is, however, a limitation of our power over slavery far more invincible than any imposed by arbitrary laws or treaties, growing out of the manner in which it is wrought into the general framework of our institutions. Putting aside all questions which relate to the origin and character of slavery, and viewing it simply under its present aspects, the prominent fact which strikes one is, that it implies a certain condition of society, — a stage of civilization, in which all — whites as well as blacks — are implicated. Were negro slavery, as seems sometimes to be thought, a mere excrescence on the surface of society, something exceptional and alien to its general structure, it might with comparative ease be removed. But instead of its being an exceptional excrescence, it is an essential and controlling element in the whole social organization of the Southern people. It penetrates through and gives color to this organization. All the laws of the South, its customs, its industrial pursuits, its social habits, are modified by slavery. The education both of home and school, the notions of what constitutes an honorable position, the respect paid to labor, the condition of the church, the moral estimates of the true ends of life, are all, more or less, determined by it. In different ways, its influence is equally decisive on the condition of the slaveholders, the non-slaveholders, and the slaves. The whites need to go through a training for freedom scarcely less than the blacks. The master is as much fettered to one end of the chain, as the slave to the other; and it would be difficult to say which is least prepared for emancipation.

It is obvious that to reconstruct the whole fabric of society — which is what is implied in any wise method of abolishing slavery — can never be the work of a day. Had the slaves been introduced a few years ago into a community whose industrial habits and social judgments and moral feelings had been formed under free institutions, they might be suddenly removed, and the transient void, soon filled, would scarcely be observed. But to change the organic life of ten millions of people, to change institutions and ideas rooted in the past and wrought into all the customs of common life, must, at the best, be a very slow and gradual process. To expunge slavery from the statute book would be the least and easiest part of what is required, — far easier, certainly, than to legislate into the minds of whites or blacks the ideas which belong to free institutions. Were legal slavery abolished at the South, it would probably be centuries before it could be abolished from the southern mind. Even at the North, the black, when equal with the white before the law, is as far as ever from having vindicated for himself any position of social equality. In England, in spite of affinities of race and color, and general equality of culture, eight centuries have hardly effaced the distinction between Norman and Saxon, and still less that between Saxon and Celt. And thus far, all experiments in emancipation, which have left the negro in the same country with his former master — for the British West Indies with the immense disproportion which exists there between whites and blacks cannot be regarded as forming any real exception — show how nearly impossible it is to overcome the barriers of race, caste, color, and historical association, so that the two parties shall meet each other on equal terms.

Such considerations show plainly enough what formidable obstacles are in the way of all attempts to remove slavery. And, what is of still more consequence, they force upon us the conviction that any change, which deserves the name of improvement, in the social condition of a people among whom slavery exists, must, from the necessity of the case, be very gradual, and must be the result, not of revolution, but of growth.

This is, in many respects, a very sad and discouraging conclusion. There is one point of view, however, which ought not to be altogether passed by, from which the picture seems to be relieved of some portion of its depth of shadow. However deep-dyed in guilt slavery may commonly have been, both in its origin and its history, there are certain conditions of society and a certain stage of progress in which, if it be an evil, it has for the slave himself many counterbalancing advantages. If the wrong in our own country has been on the side of the whites, upon them also has fallen the heaviest part of the penalty. Jefferson, thinking of the whites, said "I tremble for my country, when I reflect that

God is just." His apprehensions of the retributions of heaven are, day by day, blackening into more substantial realities. The very soil of the South is blasted by slavery, and there is not one moral or social interest which does not feel its disastrous influence. On the other hand, it can scarcely be doubted that the blacks, on the whole, have been benefited by their position. We do not mean by this that their condition might not have been more favorable than it has been; and, least of all, do we say it by way of apology for slavery. But it shows that there is an overruling Providence which educes good from evil, which makes evil correct or consume itself, and forbids it to be eternal; and, in doing this, makes us more patient with those social imperfections whose remedy is beyond our control.

The slaves of the South are, comparatively, not only a civilized people, but we doubt if, in the whole history of mankind, a single example can be adduced of a race of men starting from such a depth of moral degradation and barbarism, and in a century and a half making so vast an advance in civilization. This progress has been owing, as we believe, in no small part to the fact of their being slaves. Through this relation they have been brought into close contact with a superior race, under circumstances of restraint and excitement which have compelled them to abstain from some of the most debasing vices, to form habits of industry, and which have led them to catch rapidly the social, moral, and religious ideas of their masters. This does not extenuate the moral wrong of slavery, for it originated in no such philanthropic purpose. It is a fact, however, not to be overlooked. How great this progress has been, is seen the moment they are sent back to Africa, and placed side by side with those descended from the same general stock. The native African is still a brute, bowing before a stone, offering human sacrifices, without arts or industry, with scarcely a notion of right or wrong, a mere savage, and of the most degraded kind. The emancipated slaves who have colonized Liberia have gone far to prove themselves competent to establish and conduct — the greatest work of man on earth — a free and Christian commonwealth. They have churches, and schools, and courts of justice, and a representative government, and laws to which they know how to secure obedience. The marriage bond is as much respected, the home is as sacred, and the education of the young as anxiously provided for, as among the great mass of the people in the more civilized states of Europe. And this progress, and more than this, is the fruit of a gradual culture under a condition of slavery; and could scarcely have existed without those habits of obedience, industry, and temperance, which, if exacted by the master for his own advantage, have in the end redounded far more to the benefit of the slave. We confess that we fear, if, one hundred or one hundred and fifty years ago, any large number of native Africans had been landed in New England, and left, with their freedom, to provide for themselves, that their descendants at this moment, if any still existed, would be in a far more debased condition than if their fathers had been trained up from barbarism under the restraints of slavery.

But while this is true, and while it qualifies our regret that slavery should have existed, and while we would not be blind to the extreme difficulty of removing it from a country where it is once established, we have no idea of allowing ourselves to be regarded as its apologists or defenders. If there are circumstances under which slavery has many compensating advantages, it is equally true, that, as men gain self-control and rise above the level of savage life, slavery hinders the progress which at an earlier stage it may have helped. And here is its true evil. The great wrong does not arise out of the fact that every man possesses an absolute and perfect right to freedom. What are termed abstract rights are nearly all of them subject to great limitations and qualifications. Rights imply duties; social rights imply corresponding duties to society; and he who has no ability to perform the duties, has no just claim to the rights. So long as one is incompetent to perform the duties of a freeman, he has, properly speaking, no right to be free. But, on the contrary, there can be no greater wrong than that of which they are guilty who, for selfish ends, make use of superior power to prevent him from becoming competent to the duties and rights of freedom. If man possesses any right, it is to become what God intended him to be — a man. Here is the curse of slavery. Its continued existence depends on *preventing* in the slave the development of the higher qualities of manhood. It exists only by shutting off the slave from education, from forming habits of self-support, and, as far as possible, from all hope of a better state. It allows the slave to rise as near to manhood as it dares, because the more intelligent labor is, the more profitable; but beyond this, it systematically represses all mental or moral culture which would tend to awaken the instinct for freedom. It is not that the slave is not well fed, and clothed, and cared for, as an animal; but that the institution of slavery maintains itself by preventing his rising above a condition half-way between the animal and the man. It is not that men in other conditions do not live in ignorance and endure life-long deprivations; but that slavery is an institution which sustains itself only by systematically keeping at a degraded level those under its control, and must cease to exist were any general and serious effort made to raise the slave to a higher mental or moral level. And they who, — for the sake of their personal comfort, ease, or gain, — support, without attempting to change, an institution like this, must expect to encounter the sober reprobation of the Christian world.

But while we shall not defend slavery, we are equally far from thinking that all means, irrespective of their tendency or character, may be used for its removal. As in the case of other social evils, we wish to see no remedies applied which are worse than the disease, but those only which will change a most imperfect social state for a better one. We wish to see slavery abolished, but not by methods which will introduce in its stead worse evils than itself. Slavery is bad, but there are many things worse. A savage anarchy is infinitely worse. It is worse for the land to be under the rule of the appetites and passions of the ignorant, than under the despotic rule of the more intelligent. It is better that men should remain slaves, than be converted by the touch of freedom into idle and sensual savages. We desire to see slavery removed, but through those methods of improvement alone, which, as it disappears, shall cause a fairer order of society to take its place.

The moral sense of the world demands of the South, not that it shall abolish slavery in a day or a year, but that it shall show, by some decided action, that an institution which, it confesses, keeps the slave in a low, debased, and inferior state, it does not intend, because of its profitableness, nor for any reason but the direst necessity, to be a permanent one. Were the Southern States, with a prospective view to emancipation, to adopt some effective plan by which to educate the blacks for the duties of freedom, — were they thus, in some proper method and by intention, preparing them for its ultimate enjoyment — though the process of training the slave for freedom were as long as that which has accustomed him to the habits of bondage — it would be felt that they were meeting, as can be done in no other way, the responsibilities of their position.

And in speaking of the wrong to which the slave is subjected, and of the duty of the slaveholder, we do not think it necessary to take on us any airs of moral indignation, nor to assume the attitude of homilists. Every word we have written is assented to as heartily, and, except among the immediate disciples of Mr. Calhoun, almost as generally, at the South as at the North. The number of Slave States in which nearly successful efforts have been made to abolish slavery, the multitude of slaveholders everywhere met with, to whom slavery is a source of perpetual grief and anxiety, the kind of interest which has been taken in colonization, and the efforts to improve the lot of the black in slavery, even where no means are used to deliver him from it, show the existence of the same moral sensibility on this subject at the

South, which exists throughout the more enlightened parts of Christendom.

That slavery ought to be regarded as a temporary institution merely, and as one which every wise and good man should, according to his ability, labor to remove as far and as fast as is consistent with any real improvement in the condition of society, is a proposition which will be assented to almost as universally by the South as by the North; while few, north or south, would go beyond this in their statement of the duty to promote emancipation.

But if slavery is ever to be abolished, the question, *By whom must the work be done?*—becomes one of great moment, not only for those who are immediately responsible, that they may justly appreciate their position, but for those also who, properly speaking, are not responsible, that they may not embarrass the action of those upon whom the burden of this great enterprise must fall. It is a question which should be fairly answered, in order that between different parts of the country there may be harmony, and concert, and mutual tolerance, and a friendly willingness to give and receive aid. No good object is advanced by assuming a responsibility beyond our province. Even in promoting the best ends, we must respect each other's moral freedom, and social and civil rights.

On whom, then, so far as any direct action is concerned, are we chiefly to rely for the removal of slavery? For reasons to which we have already adverted, we cannot look to the people of the Free States. They are shut out from all authority over the subject. They have no more right or opportunity to vote in the legislature of Alabama, than in the Parliament of England; and the slave laws of the South are as far beyond their control, as the English corn laws. If this be true, it is a truth which should be fully recognized; for any action founded upon a contrary supposition can result in nothing but mischief. But to whom then can we look? We answer, to that large class of men at the South, not sufficiently regarded in our anti-slavery movements, who desire to see slavery give place to free institutions.

If slavery is ever done away by human means, unless it be through revolution, insurrection, and civil war, it must be by southern men; and the only persons who have any direct influence for good over this matter, and who can be expected voluntarily to exert that influence, are the southern friends of emancipation. Any northern method of agitating the question of slavery, which overlooks this point, must be fatally erroneous. We fear that it has been overlooked, and already with very mischievous results. We have never heard any man, acquainted with the South, doubt that the feeling in regard to the abolition of slavery, has, within the last few years, undergone a very great

change. Whatever important ends slavery agitation at the North may have accomplished, it has paralyzed and struck dumb the southern friends of freedom. Fifteen or twenty years ago, large numbers, in all parts of the South, for different reasons and in different degrees, looked with dislike on slavery, and with favor on whatever tended towards its removal. In Maryland, Virginia, and Kentucky, the emancipation party was a large and powerful one. Now it is silenced and all but annihilated. Multitudes are altogether repelled from it, while others, shrinking from a false position, recoiling from any seeming treachery to their friends and neighbors, and fearing to be identified with northern abolitionists, are silenced. We attribute this state of things in part to the influence of Mr. Calhoun, and in part to the increased value of slave property; but that state of feeling which has made the calm and fair discussion of the subject all but impossible, we attribute mainly to the manner in which it has been treated at the North. The emancipation party in the Slave States has been palsied by the action of abolitionism, more entirely even, than the Colonization Society in the Free States. A method of agitation whose main result has been to destroy that party which alone had it in its power to do any thing effectively for the abolition of slavery, seems to us a mournful one. The right of free discussion is a sacred one, and not to be surrendered; but a mode of discussion, whether in Northern Legislatures or pulpits, or in the halls of Congress, which tends to injure the cause in hand, is quite a different thing; and to call the insisting on this mode of destructive speech a vindication of the freedom of speech, or to attribute that opposition to it which has been really occasioned by a conviction of its uselessness or mischievousness, to a disregard of the value of free discussion, implies either great injustice or a melancholy confusion of ideas.

But if we are to wait for the growth of an emancipation party at the South, it is said, we may wait a century before it is large enough to accomplish any thing. This may be so, or not. It does not, however, alter the fact, that it is the only human agency, except it be through violence, to which we can look for the removal of slavery. We have in this case, as in so many others, to trust for the good which we desire, to the slow development of causes over which we have but little control. It is certain that our impatience will do little to hasten the social progress of States in the management of whose internal affairs we have no voice; while our uninvoked interference will only cripple the action of those who alone have the disposition and power to promote the welfare of the blacks.

But are there no causes at work to remove slavery besides those dependent on human choice, — Providential causes, wrought into the

general tendencies of society? We believe that there are, and that they will finally raise the slave to the level of a free man.

The first is what may be termed the spirit of the age. For a hundred years, in large portions of Europe and throughout this country, there has been a steady progress towards free institutions, and an increasing respect for the rights of the individual man. It is a spirit which has manifested itself in all the struggles of the people against the despotisms of the older world. It has promoted education. It has transformed despotisms into constitutional governments, which, leaving the individual under the obligation, has secured for him the protection, of law. It has abolished the slave trade. It has caused the powerful and prosperous to pay infinitely greater attention to the condition of the poor and wretched. And this spirit of the age, breathed in through all the thought and literature of the time, is felt and will be felt by the slaveholder as it is by others. It leads him involuntarily to pay more regard to the individual rights of the slave. Its influence is seen in the increased amount of religious instruction which the slaves receive, and in their generally improved condition in regard to the essential matters of food, clothing, and labor. It is an invisible agency which cannot be shut out by State lines or laws; it penetrates into the mind of the master, and makes him familiar with ideas against which he may rebel, but which he cannot cast out; it kindles up new and inspiring hopes in the mind of the slave, and bears all on, with the sure progress of the tides, towards freedom.

The second cause is one which is felt particularly by the border States. A slight inspection of the returns of the last census shows that these States are silently, but certainly, passing through a social revolution. Whatever the causes may be, it is obvious that slavery is retiring, step by step, towards the South, and that the present tendency is for it to become accumulated there in one solid mass. The whole population of the northern tier of Slave States — Delaware, Maryland, District of Columbia, Virginia, Kentucky, Missouri — in 1830, was 2,603,389. In 1840, it was 2,995,143; and in 1850, it was 3,832,430. In the same States, the slave population, by the census of 1830, was 771,756. In 1840, it was 786,-521; and in 1850, it was 879,859. Without entering into other particulars, we have here the fact, a mere statement of which stands in the place of all general reasonings on the subject — that while the population of these border States during the twenty years between 1830 and 1850, had increased 1,229,041, the number of slaves had increased only 108,103. Thus, while the slave population has remained nearly stationary, the white population has increased more than a million; or to be more precise, while the whole population has advanced at the rate of about 50 per cent., the slaves have increased only 14 per cent., during the last twenty years. The more one examines the progress of the individual States, the more striking will these facts appear. This relative decrease of the slave population is not owing to any diminution in the per centage of births, as compared with that of the whites, but to the fact that it has shrunk and withered away on its northern border. Year by year, it is receding towards the South. Slave property on the border becomes of almost no value; and the slaves who remain there, and whose masters intend that they shall remain, are practically, to no small extent, losing the character and emerging above the condition of slaves. Whatever may be said morally of the internal slave trade, the result is a very obvious one. It is draining the northern tier of Slave States of its slaves, and transferring them to the South. As their numbers increase, unless the space which they occupy is also enlarged, their value will diminish. The black population will outgrow the white, and Alabama and Texas will exhibit a counterpart of that state of things which now exists in Kentucky and Virginia. It is by no means impossible that the time may come when white laborers will very generally leave the South, and white masters become absentees, till at length, as De Tocqueville supposes to be not at all improbable, a black kingdom shall have slowly and silently established itself on the shores of the Mexican Gulf.

We have already spoken of the progress made by the blacks in civilization; we add, that as they become more civilized, they demand, and have conceded to them under the imperfect law of custom, a larger number of rights. It does not follow, because one is a slave, that he loses all the privileges of a human being. Whatever he may be in law, he is not in fact a chattel, nor is he treated as a chattel, but as a man. The word *slave* does not imply one invariable condition, any more than the word *subject*, when applied to the inhabitants of different monarchies, means always the same thing. Nor does it imply that the slave is an outlaw. In this country, the slave is protected in important rights by the law, and in still more is he protected by that public sentiment which creates and gives authority to law. As he becomes more capable of freedom, although his nominal condition may remain the same, he is generally found to possess more freedom. It is difficult not to treat men to a considerable degree in accordance with what they really are. When an Irishman from Cork or Connaught first lands here, just dug out of his bog, the mud of his cabin still thick and hard upon him, stultified, cowed down, not more ignorant than dull, and bearing all the marks of stupidity in his face, he is of necessity treated as if he were what he is, scarcely more than an unreasoning animal. A few years pass. He receives kindness, and learns to put confidence in the good purposes of those around him. The desire of improvement is awakened, the elements of manhood are quickened, his manner becomes more free, and his features light up with dawning intelligence. He is a changed and improved man, and involuntarily the treatment which he receives undergoes a corresponding change. He may nominally hold the same place, but while the name is unaltered, his social position, in essential respects, is altogether different. So with the slaves. Those, especially, who reside near the frontier of freedom, are incessantly breathing in influences which make them more intelligent and self-relying. And, rising as men nearer to a level with their masters, their whole treatment is more or less modified. A change is in progress, similar in many respects to that through which the serfs of the Middle Ages were liberated from their feudal tyrants, and from villeins transformed into free men. We do not suppose that this cause alone will lead to emancipation; but whether the masters desire it or not, from the necessity of the case, up to a certain point, a process of improvement among the slaves must go on; through their connection with the whites and free colored persons, they cannot fail to become more intelligent, more conscious of their individual rights, and more aware of their own numbers and power; — and this cannot take place without materially modifying the character of slavery, though its name may remain.

Another consideration is to be taken into the account, in calculating the duration and fortunes of slavery. The introduction of the culture of cotton into the Southern States, and the improvements in the methods for its manufacture, increased the value of slave property, and gave an immense impulse to the growth of this institution. In most cases, the great revolutions of society are brought about far less by statesmen and soldiers, than by what seem the almost accidental changes in the agriculture, commerce, or manufactures of States. The next change which affects the South is quite as likely to be unfavorable, as favorable, to slavery. If the efforts to introduce the culture of cotton into Africa, Australia, or India, succeed, if it should be found practicable to substitute flax to any considerable extent for cotton, should some new fabric or method of manufacture be adopted, it might so seriously diminish the value of the unelastic labor of the South, that slavery would be felt to be an intolerable burden. When one remembers how rapidly such changes occur — that, within a hundred years, the great manufacturing and commercial interests of society have been almost revolutionized, that coffee and tea, whose production and importation now employ hundreds of thousands of men and large fleets, a century since were hardly used in this country or in Europe, that garments were composed of materials into which cotton for the most part did not enter, that at every short period some new article of agriculture or commerce is introduced — like that of opium in India — on which the fortunes of kingdoms speedily depend, we may easily anticipate changes which will do as much to break down slavery, as the cultivation of cotton has done to build it up.

There are other facts of still greater significance, because they indicate that, throughout the country, there is a prevailing and powerful tendency of feeling and opinion towards emancipation. We doubt if its extent is at all appreciated. We are not conscious of the forward movement, because, like ships sailing on parallel lines, all move together. At successive periods between the years 1780 and 1804, seven States passed laws for the abolition of slavery, thus anticipating, by many years, and at quite as great relative sacrifices, the similar action of the English Parliament in regard to the West Indies. From the Northwestern Territory, and at a time when no additions of territory beyond this were looked for by any one, it was excluded by the organic law under which the States formed out of this region came into the Union; and it should not be forgotten that this law received, with one exception, the unanimous vote of the Continental Congress by which it was enacted. Into a large part of the recently acquired territory it is not, and is not likely to be, admitted. And all this has happened, not accidentally, but as the result of settled and well-considered convictions. In the mean time, the foreign slave trade has been abolished; in several of the remaining Slave States strenuous efforts have been made to prepare the way for emancipation; throughout the South, the question of emancipation is brought into perpetual discussion; the extension of slavery has been limited; and at the present time, the legislatures of various States, both north and south, show a disposition to promote the colonization of free blacks, or of those who may be liberated for that purpose.

More important, however, than any of these facts, in the way of showing the tendency of things, is the number of *free blacks*. At the close of the Revolution, there were scarcely any in the country. The words, negro and slave, were regarded as nearly equivalent. By the last census, the number of free blacks, is 418,173. These, wherever found, have all been slaves or are the descendants of slaves. Those born at the North were emancipated by law. But of the whole number, the larger part, — 233,691 — are still found at the South; and they, or their parents, and large numbers besides, who have left the South, have been liberated by the individual humanity of their owners. Where so many masters, in spite of the many hinderances in the way, have given to their slaves their freedom, a far greater number must be strongly inclined to take the same step. The laws interpose many obstacles in the way of any individual who wishes to emancipate his slaves; and public opinion, which, at the North as well as at the South, dooms those who are emancipated to the wretched condition of a subordinate caste, interposes more obstacles. Humane men, who are conscious of just and kind purposes towards those under their control, naturally hesitate long before they throw their slaves in their weakness and dependence, some of them young and some old, upon their own resources, under such unfavorable circumstances. We think that those at all acquainted with the South would say, that, in a multitude of cases, it is the humanity of the masters which causes them to retain their slaves in bondage. If, under these circumstances, so many are made free, it shows clearly enough, not only how strong and deep is the sentiment which sets towards emancipation, but that it exists in scarcely less strength at the South than at the North.

The first of August, 1838, is memorable throughout the world, as the day on which eight hundred thousand human beings in the British West Indies had the shackles of the slave struck from their limbs and were restored to their rights as men. It was a great day for mankind,—one of those historical days which measure the progress of the human race. And yet the West Indian slaves, instead of being liberated by their masters, owed their freedom to the votes of a Parliament which held its sittings three thousand miles across the ocean, and in which the masters were not represented. England generously contributed £20,000,000 as a partial compensation for the slaves, which burden fell, in the shape of an increase to the public debt, on a large and rich nation; but a far larger pecuniary loss, as such property is reckoned, fell upon the slaveholder. Far be it from us to detract from the merits of this great event, whose nobleness lights up the dark track of history, and must be an inspiring example to all times. The world cannot afford to forget it. But let us remember that, if the emancipation of the slaves in the West Indies, by an act of the British Parliament, was a triumph of the philanthropy of England, similar acts of emancipation by the legislatures of the northern States, years before, and the liberation by their immediate owners of so many slaves at the South, are not less decided proofs of the philanthropy of America. Under the circumstances, the existence of more than 400,000 free blacks in the United States, who owe their freedom to the free choice of those who were the immediate owners of themselves or their fathers, is a far more unquestionable evidence of a wide-spread humanity and desire for the emancipation of the blacks, than the 800,000 liberated slaves of the West Indies.*

These circumstances, and others of a similar kind, show a steady tendency — not a casual spasm, but a tendency created by the industrial relations, the social theories, and the moral sentiments most characteristic of the times — towards the abolition of slavery. We cannot doubt that sooner or later it will be swept from the land.

But whether emancipation will, within any calculable period, result in any decided good to whites or blacks, we think a much more unsettled point. The South is in one of those Serbonian bogs, in which the peril seems almost equally great to go forward or back. The result must, apparently, depend in no small degree on the manner in which the abolition of slavery is accomplished. If, as is quite too possible, "the area of freedom" is enlarged by the "annexation" of the rest of Mexico to the United States, the blacks will continue to recede towards the tropics. Crowded down into the isthmus, and into a climate favorable to them and fatal to the whites, the time may come in the revolutions of the world, when, constituting a State by themselves, they may, like a pear which is ripe, drop off, or be separated by violence from the United States. Should this occur, their subsequent fortunes must, under Providence, depend on themselves. If the two races, after the slaves are set free, remain together at the South, we can foresee nothing but evil. If amalgamation should take place, it would create a third race, certainly inferior to the white, and

---

*The cordial invitation from England to America to participate in the "World's Fair," has had one drawback. Not only has the periodical press, from the Quarterly to the daily newspaper, been abundant in admonitions, but leading men in different religious bodies, among other acts of a similar kind, have gone so far as to give us warning, that no American ministers of the gospel can expect to be admitted to their pulpits or their private hospitality, except those who adopt the general views of the abolitionists. Of course, the English people have an entire right to determine for themselves what rules they will be governed by in their intercourse with strangers, and being fairly warned, it will be their own fault if the proscribed classes do not avoid personal insult; but on the whole, a less inhospitable and objurgatory benevolence would better accord with some of the antecedents of English history. It is not now for the first time that we have had experience of the willingness of England to superintend and direct the course of this country in regard to slavery. Besides the facts referred to above, there are others worth remembering. Not only was slavery *forced* on this country by England, against the all but unintermitted resistance of the Colonies, but in repeated cases, the Provincial legislatures passed laws to hinder or prevent the introduction of slaves, without being able to obtain for them the sanction of the royal governors or the British crown. In abolishing the slave trade, this country from the beginning took the lead of England. Though not extinguished till 1808, several of the individual States, immediately after the Revolution, among others, Virginia, prohibited the slave trade to their citizens; and from 1794, the records of Congress show repeated enactments all looking to the same end. This country was equally in advance of England in regard to emancipation. For two years preceding the case of the slave Somersett in England, and in defiance of the whole system of Colonial administration, the Courts of Massachusetts had granted liberty to slaves suing their masters for freedom, on principles of right quite as broad as those which controlled the decision of Lord Mansfield. After the Revolution, the northern States, by successive acts, emancipated the slaves within their borders; and from that day to this, in spite of exceptional cases, and in spite of whatever resistance may have been from time to time opposed to it, the steady tendency of things has been towards the final abolition of slavery.

probably inferior to the negro. But there is no reason to anticipate an amalgamation. It is far more likely to take place while they are slaves, than after they are free. The moment the slave is liberated, the lines of caste will be more tightly drawn; and living in the presence of their former masters, and amidst the associations of servitude, they will always continue to be mere hewers of wood and drawers of water. This is the best fate for which they can look. There is another result, of whose possibility history gives us warning. It is, a war of races, in which the feebler race will be crushed down into a more hopeless state, till, losing all courage and energy, it gradually perishes out of existence.

Is there no way of anticipating and preventing these evils? In general, they will be averted, or modified and softened, in the same degree that society, white and black, is thoroughly christianized and brought into a state in which every man shall first of all strive to do justly, to love mercy, and to walk humbly before God. But of specific remedies we know only one, and that is *colonization*. Even this, at the best, as we are quite ready to concede, must be a very imperfect and gradual one; it may never prove fully competent to meet the exigencies of the case; but so far as we can perceive, it is on this, more than on any thing else, that the black race must rely for any speedy improvement in its condition.

When the subject of colonization is proposed, the first question to be answered relates to its feasibility. Is it to such an extent practicable, that we may hope by means of it to make any real impression on the condition of the blacks in this country? The past history and present prospects of Liberia show plainly enough that it would be for the benefit of the blacks, if, under proper circumstances, they could be established in Africa. At any rate, if they cannot, when there, maintain themselves in a state of comparative freedom and civilization, it is very certain that in this country, in the presence of a more energetic race, they cannot hope to rise above the level of a servile caste. But under any circumstances, is it possible to transport them to Africa in such numbers as to warrant our regarding this measure as a means of improving the condition of the blacks, or of promoting the abolition of slavery?

Within the last few years, we have had new and important experiences in this matter of colonization. Some three hundred thousand persons are now annually transported from Ireland to America. At the same rate, the whole slave population might be transferred to Africa in twenty years. Germany is sending its people to our shores, almost by provinces. From our Atlantic coasts, emigrants are moving in columns of tens of thousands to the West. The Mormons, after traversing the intervening desert, are building up an empire in the interior of the continent; while the coasts of the Pacific are becoming populous with the advancing hosts of civilization. Nor is this confined to the United States alone. Impelled by want, by ambition, by a hot and restless spirit of enterprise, immense armies are leaving the older world to plant themselves in Canada, Australia, New Zealand, Southern Africa, and India. The whole world is in movement; and of the innumerable emigrants whose fleets, setting in all directions, cross each other's tracks on every sea, the far greater proportion leave home under as hard conditions, and go to confront as serious difficulties, as any which the free black who emigrates to Africa is called on to encounter. Such facts as these, to say the least, take African colonization out of the circle of impossibilities.

There is another view, which shows that there is nothing absolutely impracticable in the simple transportation of them across the seas. During the last ten years, the whole black population of the United States, slave and free, has increased at the average rate of not quite 75,000 annually. To show what rapid changes are within the bounds of possibility, the removal of 100,000 annually from the United States would, in twenty-five years, — a short time in the history of a nation — not only prevent any increase of the slave population, but would reduce it from twenty to twenty-five per cent. below its present number. In the mean while, the white population would have doubled itself, and such a change have taken place in the relative numbers of the two races as to make slavery a comparatively manageable evil.

The expense may be great, but properly conducted, it need not be such as to weigh heavily on the finances of this country. By the Treaty of Washington, we are obliged to support on the coast of Africa a squadron of some eighty guns, at a great cost of money and health and life. Were the sum expended on this slender coast-guard, which certainly does not seem to realize the expectations originally formed of it, applied to colonization, or were the two objects, as they might easily be, combined, it would not only do infinitely more to annihilate the slave trade, but would probably supply the means for carrying emigrants to Africa, as rapidly as is at present desirable.

But there is no reason for supposing that the whole expense would fall on the Government. If these African colonies prosper, and the blacks become satisfied that Africa opens to them and their children better prospects than America, a new state of things will soon exist. The African trade, already an important one, will be constantly enlarging and increasing in value. The commercial relations between America and Liberia will become more close. Commerce opens and makes easy the way, and provides the means and facilities, for emigration. As the ships engaged in the trade of the two countries become more numerous, the opportunities for procuring a passage will increase. The number of free blacks is already large; and any great diminution in the value of slave labor, in connection with other causes to which we have referred, is likely to make it much larger; while in general, they will easily find the means to pay the expenses of emigration. Each prosperous emigrant will become a centre of attraction to the little circle of friends whom he has left behind in this country. Those now free are not more destitute than the Irish; and as soon as they are satisfied that Liberia holds out a reasonable assurance to them of prosperity and comfort, they will find their way thither through some of the multiplied avenues of a constantly growing intercourse. When it becomes evident that the colony is established on a firm basis, and that it opens profitable opportunities for the investment of capital and the employment of industry, and when the state of the schools and churches is such as to secure to society the religious instruction which it needs, and to the young the means of education, the fortunes of Liberia may be safely left to the ordinary laws on which the growth of communities depends. If any foreign aid should be needed, the recent action of not less than five or six legislatures of different States shows that it will be easily obtained.

We make these statements, not because we think it desirable that so large a mass of emigrants should, in the present state of things, be thrown at once on the African coast, but to show that the simple transportation of the blacks to the land of their origin presents, in itself, no insurmountable difficulties. So rapid a change as we have imagined is not to be desired or expected. It has taken two centuries to bring slavery into its present state; and we may be well satisfied if the ascent from this Avernus is not longer than the descent.

But to all such projects, it is replied, that the invincible obstacle in the way of their accomplishment lies in the pecuniary value of the slaves to their owners. The slaveholders will not make the enormous sacrifice of property which emancipation involves, nor will the United States government assume the burden of this sacrifice. Of course, this objection does not apply to the colonization of free blacks, nor to those who may hereafter be made free; but only to colonization as a method of emancipation. We acknowledge, however, the full force of this difficulty. If no other causes were at work tending to relieve the country of slavery except colonization, we should consider the matter hopeless. But this by no means presents a full view of the case.

The ground which we take is this: — that there are powerful and irresistible influences at work in a large part of the Slave States, tending towards the abolition of slavery within their boundaries; — that colonization coöperates harmoniously with these tendencies; — that, in removing those who become free to Africa, it is conferring an inestimable good on the blacks; and, in so doing, it relieves these States of a class whose presence, wisely or unwisely, causes the South to look with dread on emancipation, as ultimately full of danger both to blacks and whites. This point is of so much importance that we will illustrate by an example what the practical relations of a wise and large scheme of colonization would be to emancipation.

If slavery is ever abolished, it will be gradually, and first of all, in the Slave States on the northern border. We may take the case of Maryland, to explain what is very likely to be the progress of events. The whole number of slaves in Maryland, in 1830, was 102,294. In 1840, it was 89,737. In 1850, it was 89,800. Thus, through the agency of causes now at work, during the last twenty years, there has been an actual falling off, in the slave population, of 12,494. In the mean time, the population of the State has increased 135,466, amounting by the census of 1850, to 582,506. Thus, while the number of slaves is diminishing, the white population is steadily increasing, and through this increasing disproportion between the two races, slavery is every day coming more and more under control. Besides, as is evident from the circumstance that so many are set free, there are large numbers of slaveholders disinclined to hold slave property, and equally disinclined to sell their slaves. Of these, some would be glad to liberate their slaves at once; and many more, unwilling to leave them in bondage, would liberate them at death, could they have any assurance that their condition would be changed for the better. Were the United States Government, — adopting some plan like that suggested by Mr. Webster in his speech of March 7, 1850 — and which it appears from his remarks was formerly suggested, we believe, by Rufus King — (one of those gigantic plans which contemporaries reject as impracticable, and which posterity admires as characterized by a prophetic sagacity) — to engage to transport to Africa as many as should be set free for that purpose, and to provide them with the means of support for a reasonable time after their arrival, there is every ground for believing that many now retained in bondage would be liberated. Through this decrease of the slave population, and the corresponding increase in the number of intelligent and influential non-slaveholders — for such is likely to be the character of those who voluntarily liberate their slaves — the whole aspect of slavery must be changed; and in a few years, the state of things is likely to be such as to lead to its entire and voluntary abolition. Similar causes would tend to produce similar results in the whole northern tier of Slave States ; while each State which becomes free, must, in so doing, aid powerfully that course of events which is leading on towards universal emancipation.

But granting that it is impossible, even if it be desirable, to transport all the blacks of this country to Africa ; still any wise and comprehensive system of colonization must have a deep and wide influence on the institution of slavery. The scattered settlements, from Sierra Leone to the San Pedro, have already annihilated the slave trade along that extended line of coast, which was formerly the favorite resort of the slave-trader. If the blacks prove themselves to be capable of freedom, and succeed in establishing and maintaining free institutions, they will take from the defenders of slavery one strong argument derived from the assumed inferiority of the negro race. Free, civilized, and prosperous commonwealths cannot be built up in Africa, without awaking in the blacks of this country new hopes and ambitions. They will rise in their own estimation and in that of the whites. One reason why we so readily acquiesce in the existence of slavery is, that we are accustomed, both North and South, to see the blacks occupy subordinate positions. The existence in Africa of self-supporting States, founded by emancipated slaves, cannot fail to react on the public sentiment of this country, and to modify the general estimate in which slavery is held, while it must go far to break up the habit of associating the blacks with a depressed and degraded condition.

Except as a matter of humanity, the white population of the North has no direct interest in colonization. The blacks are not sufficiently numerous to enable them to make their influence felt. They herd together in the larger towns, and are generally employed as domestic servants, cooks, stewards on board of vessels, barbers, petty dealers, or in some similar subordinate, but useful, positions. As a class, they are orderly and industrious, and in these respects, in no way inferior to the great mass of foreign emigrants.

It is far different, however, with the Southern States. In removing the free blacks, that part of the population is removed which is likely to furnish the intelligent leaders of insurrections, and whose simple presence, by keeping before the slaves the visible possibility of freedom, is the perpetual source among them of irritation and uneasiness. Colonies and colonization may thus look for support from the South, as a matter of interest. But far more than on this, we rely on Southern humanity ; — not on vague professions, but on that humane consideration of the slaves manifested in their improved condition and in the numbers now set free, and which, fostered by Christianity and by all the social tendencies of the times, must yearly gain strength and power.

For the blacks, bond and free, colonization is so desirable, that without it, the gift of freedom would be robbed of half its privilege. Sure we are, that if those now free, or hereafter to be made free, should, as the condition under which liberty was to be enjoyed, be required not to leave the country, it would be deemed, by the best friends of the colored race, a wrong and an injury second only to absolute bondage. Our legislatures would be thronged with petitioners, and the air would be fevered with the indignant eloquence of those demanding, for the black, permission to emigrate to some land where he might seek his fortune under more propitious omens. And with good reason. At the South, the condition of the negro, even when set free, is always a degraded one, and at the North, scarcely less so; nor is there any prospect of any material change in his condition for the better. We certainly do not defend, or apologize for, this state of things; but it exists, and none are more conscious of it than the blacks themselves. Without dwelling on the causes of it, every intelligent black feels that, in this country, he can never be more than half a man. We honor those who strive to rise above this depressing lot, and our deepest sympathies go with them in their struggles against what seems to be an inevitable doom. But, practically, it is a struggle without hope. The black man withers under the shadow of the white. It proceeds in part, as we cannot help thinking, from some undefined difference of race. But whether so or not, the circumstance that the two races have stood together in the relation of master and slave, has modified all their estimates of each other, and after the black is protected in every right by law, the influence of this fact, as subtle as it is powerful, still keeps him in bondage. In Africa, surrounded by those of his own color, taken out of that charmed circle within which, though nominally free, he is still a slave, he becomes really emancipated. He assumes the responsibilities, undertakes the enterprises, and relies on that self-guidance and support, which develop the higher faculties and qualities of the man. He becomes altogether a different being. If Liberia grows up into a settled, self-sustaining commonwealth, her people will associate on equal terms with those of equal culture in every part of the world.

In urging these schemes of colonization, the common objection made to them is, that they are unrighteous and cruel. We do not acquiesce in the justice of this charge. There is certainly no want of humanity in the purposes of those most active in promoting colonization. As a matter of fact, the blacks in this country occupy an unhappy social position. There is not only no prospect of great improvement, but those who declaim most loudly against the wrong done the negro race, are as little ready as any to take the only step — amalgamation — which, by blending the races together, can ever afford any thing like an effectual remedy. The most zealous abolitionists would hesitate long before encouraging intermarriage between their children and those of the blacks. We believe that, in this respect, their instincts are better than their reasonings. We do not believe that amalgamation is desirable for either race. We believe that the difference of races which Providence established, it is well to maintain. But whether so or not, there is no probability of complete amalgamation, while without it, the circumstances which now depress the free black will continue to depress him. In defending colonization, we are not excusing prejudice or injustice. We simply recognize facts which we have not power to change, and which, if ever removed, are more likely than in any other way, to be so, by its being shown on the part of the blacks, that they are capable of supporting a civilized government of their own. Under these circumstances, we think it the part of humanity to aid them in placing themselves where their situation is likely to be more favorable for all their true interests, than they can hope it to be in this country.

The rhetorical statement, that colonization is a scheme by which the black is to be expelled from his native country, does not greatly affect us. It is not a new thing in the world for men to remove to distant lands for the purpose of improving their condition, and there is very little cruelty in aiding them so to do. It is to be remembered that, so far as the free blacks are concerned, they are not asked to emigrate except in accordance with their own choice : and as to the slaves, if liberty be a boon of any value, they can scarcely be thought to do them an injury, who besides setting them free, establish them, without expense on their part, in a free commonwealth of their own color and race. At this moment, constrained by the pressure of infelicitous circumstances, or to improve their fortunes, hundreds of thousands of Europeans are annually driven, or impelled to leave, their own country for America. Under the circumstances, we do not think them unwise in seeking a home on our shores, or that the destitute among their number are injured or wronged by those friends who encourage and aid them to embark. If there is cruelty, it is on the part of those German governments which endeavor by hard restrictions and needless obstacles, to prevent their subjects from leaving. Among us, they are doing the same poor work, who, by appealing to the prejudices, the jealousies, and the fears of the blacks, are hindering them from seeking a home where, under better auspices, they and their children may be really free.

Were it the question whether it would be wise to emigrate to an entirely new and unsettled country, — though multitudes of the Anglo-Saxon race are not deterred from penetrating through the gates of the Rocky Mountains and making a home in the wilds of Oregon, — we might hesitate as to the answer. But the first difficulties of African colonization are overcome. Liberia, including the Maryland colony, extends from the river San Pedro to Sherbro, a distance of more than 500 miles. The civilized population is estimated at 7,000 or 8,000, while the heathen population, in the territory over which it has acquired the right of jurisdiction, is above 200,000. The soil is fertile, the exports have risen to half a million annually, and are rapidly increasing, while new forms of industry are developing new resources. The republic of Liberia is not yet four years old; but Great Britain and France have already entered into diplomatic relations with it. The blacks are proving their capacity to form and sustain a free state by every evidence which the circumstances admit. They have organized the whole framework of government; and President Roberts has exhibited a force of mind and character which shows his entire competency to be at the head of this great enterprise. In their churches, they have more than 2000 communicants, and more than 1500 children in sabbath schools. The laws provide for a common school in every town, and in these, where they are established, or in the day schools attached to the various missions, are not less than 1200 pupils. Several high schools are already opened; and the attempt is now making among the friends of the colony in this country, and with every prospect of success, to raise means for the establishment of a college, in which teachers and others who require a more advanced kind of instruction, may be educated. Doubtless, many things are still wanting which it is desirable to have; but the first and great difficulties, encountered in planting the colony, have been overcome, and the emigrant finds the country in some degree prepared for his reception, finds not only cultivated fields and villages and opportunities for profitable industry, but churches and schools and the institutions and resources of a comparatively settled and organized community.

It is a great incidental recommendation to this scheme of colonization, to which we have not even alluded, that it furnishes, probably the most efficient means for the regeneration of Africa. Throughout the modern world, the labors of missionaries have been paralyzed from the want of teachers of the same race with those taught. It is found next to impossible for an alien race to make any impression on the ignorant and prejudiced mass of heathenism. At all the principal missionary stations, the first step is to establish schools in which the young may from childhood grow up into the ideas, the tastes, and the habits which characterize a Christian civilization; and it is on the few, thus taught, that the chief reliance is placed for the diffusion of the Gospel and the arts and culture of civilized life among their brethren.

That class of persons which missionary societies have endeavored with very imperfect success to create, we have here at our hand, and in numbers beyond the dreams of missionary enthusiasm. Some thousands of men and women, the most ignorant of them accustomed, in an imperfect degree at least, to the ways of thinking, the manners, and the industrial arts of civilization in the midst of which they grew up, and receiving the Christian religion as the supreme rule of faith and practice, are planted in communities strong enough to protect themselves along the western coast of Africa. Connected with Christendom by all their mental and moral habits, they are connected still more closely with the native African by the powerful and permanent bond of race. The territory subject to their jurisdiction contains a native population which is already beginning to be brought under the influence of their schools and laws. Besides this, the way is opening for commercial intercourse with the whole interior of Africa. Had one, in some summer-day dream, busied himself with imagining the best method for civilizing a continent, he would have probably constructed in his fancy some such scheme as this, which, through the labors of the Colonization Society, has already become a substantive reality. It was a glorious conception, this of making emancipated slaves the regenerators of the dark land from which their fathers came. Nor has it proved to be a visionary enterprise, but one which for more than thirty years has been steadily advancing towards successful issues. Many might reasonably, at the outset, have hesitated and doubted long, before engaging in such an undertaking. But who, now that its success and promise are before the world, will not bid it God-speed? The whole cost of colonization, since its first commencement in 1817 is estimated at no more than $1,250,000; — a sum not sufficient to build and maintain for half-a-dozen years the small and comparatively ineffective squadron which we now keep on the African coast. On what enterprise during the present century has the same sum been expended, with a reasonable prospect of such great results?

Our remarks, thus far, have been almost exclusively confined to the subject of colonization in Africa. And no doubt, if colonization be looked to as a means of relieving the United States from the colored race, or if we regard the welfare of the one hundred and fifty millions of Africa, or the bearing of colonization upon the general fortunes of slavery, the coast of Liberia presents by far the most important opening for the establishment of these new commonwealths of freemen.

But at the present moment, the British West Indies offer advantageous prospects to colored immigrants; and public attention having been but little directed to these islands as a place for the settlement of the blacks, we shall venture upon certain details which would otherwise not be required. We confine ourselves to an account of Jamaica,

3

as being not only by far the largest of these islands, but the one respecting which we have the most satisfactory information. For our facts and statistics we rely on the work by Mr. Bigelow, "Jamaica in 1850," whose title we have given above. The book seems to have been very carefully prepared, by a man of sound sense and good powers of observation.

There are two principal questions which need to be answered; — first, What inducements are offered for the emigration of the free blacks to this island; and secondly, What obstacles are in the way to deter them from emigrating.

Jamaica is situated within the tropics, but the climate has the reputation of being a salubrious one, and especially so for the colored race. Indeed, the mountainous character of the interior furnishes to the settler almost any variety of climate that he may choose. The soil is so fertile as to make the island the gem of the sea. It contains about four million acres of land, of which, it is said, there are not probably any ten lying adjacent to each other which are not susceptible of the highest cultivation, while not more than five hundred thousand acres have ever been reclaimed, or even appropriated. Vegetation is never suspended, planting and harvesting go on throughout the year, and the soil is of such fertility that, notwithstanding the wretched system of cultivation, such a thing as an exhausted estate is hardly known. Fruits of all kinds are abundant, and each month has a harvest of its own. Indian corn grows luxuriantly, while potatoes, yams, cassava, peas and beans of every variety, all the common table vegetables of the United States, besides those of the tropics are easily cultivated. The island abounds in spices, drugs, and dye-stuffs of the greatest value. The crops of pimento have amounted sometimes to seven or eight million pounds a year; and yet it is said there is not a pimento-walk on the island which has been cultivated from seed planted by human hands. Among the trees are the bread-fruit tree, the cedar, the cotton-tree, the bamboo, the trumpet-tree, black and green ebony, lignumvitæ, the palmetto, and the mahogany. Its mineral wealth has been little explored, but it is thought that its copper and coal mines would prove very productive. Some parishes of the island require irrigation during a portion of the year; but in general, the island abounds with streams, and the water-power is sufficient to manufacture every thing produced by the soil, or consumed by the inhabitants. On the coast are sixteen secure harbors, and not less than thirty bays, all affording good anchorage.

But owing to the indolence of the inhabitants, to the fact that a large part of the cultivated soil has been owned by absentees, to the wretched management of their estates, to the expensive character of slave labor, and to a variety of other causes on which it is needless here to dwell, the island has sunk into utter decay and dilapidation. The sugar and coffee plantations are deserted and running to weeds. The large estates are encumbered with mortgages beyond their value. The little industry which appears is of the most inartificial, negligent, and unproductive kind; while on an island capable of producing nearly every thing which grows out of the earth, scarcely any thing is cultivated but three or four principal staples. While it might be made a garden to which the less fortunate inhabitants of other regions should resort for their supplies, its people are dependent on others for the common necessaries of life. Not a water-wheel is in use on the island, except on plantations and for agricultural purposes. Every thing is expensive; — flour from twelve to eighteen dollars a barrel; butter, thirty-seven and a half cents per pound; hams, twenty-five cents per pound; lumber, twenty-five dollars a thousand; and yet, while the island is covered with magnificent forests, there is not a saw-mill upon it. Their lumber is all imported. Their brick they import. There are no manufactories, excepting those of sugar and rum. In 1849, to refer but to a few articles, this poverty-stricken island imported, in round numbers, 70,000 barrels of flour, 87,000 bushels of corn, 17,000 barrels of pork, nearly 60,000 boxes of herrings, mackerel, and alewives, and 91,000 quintals of codfish, although the waters around the island abound in fish. Over four millions of lumber were imported, and four millions five hundred thousand of cypress and cedar shingles. And yet, all, or nearly all, these productions might be raised on the island itself, with less labor and expense, and would cost less, than in those countries from which they are chiefly received.

And, in the mean time, land has fallen to an almost nominal value. Mr. Bigelow says, "that prepared land, as fine as any under cultivation on the island, may be readily bought in unlimited quantities for five dollars an acre, while land far more productive than any in New England may be readily had at from fifty cents to a dollar." He gives an account of the sale of different estates, for the purpose of showing the present value of land. One estate of 1244 acres, which had been sold once for £18,000 sterling, was sold in 1845 for £1000. Another estate, of 1450 acres, once worth £68,000 sterling, is rated now at less than £5,000. Another estate, of 1200 acres, was sold in 1846 for £620 sterling, including machinery and works; and these are but samples which show the general condition of the island. Lands as productive as those of the Miami valley or the western prairies can, in many cases, be bought for a dollar an acre, and in most cases at a cheaper rate than in the cultivated portions of the West.

Such facts as these, of which large numbers are given in the work to which we have referred, show that industry directed by intelligence could scarcely be exerted under circumstances which promise more profitable returns. The immediate reason why the island is so unproductive is the wretched management of the large estates, the general thriftlessness and idleness of the inhabitants, the small number of productions which are cultivated, the consequent dependence on importations from abroad, and the extremely rude and clumsy instruments and methods of cultivation.

Under such circumstances, it would seem as if any intelligent and industrious colored man who should emigrate to Jamaica, possessing means wherewith to purchase a small farm, might, if he should keep up his habits of industry, in a very short time be prosperous and independent.

But such a person, before emigrating, would reasonably wish to know whether the change, in a social point of view, would be to his own advantage, or to that of his children. This question can be best answered by a reference to facts. The island is estimated to contain a population of 400,000, of which but 16,000 are white, and of the remaining 384,000 inhabitants, 68,529 are colored, and 293,128 are blacks. The Emancipation Act was passed in 1833; entire emancipation took place, August, 1838. Since that time, the blacks have enjoyed the same political privileges as the whites, and have shared with them the honors and patronage of government. As a necessary consequence of this, and of the immense numerical preponderance of the black population, it seems even that a diminished, though doubtless still a great, importance is attached to complexion. Intermarriages between the white and colored people are frequent; and where there is equality in other respects, although very much of the ancient prejudice in favor of the whites may remain, no social distinctions, based exclusively on color, are recognized. Colored people are received at the Governor's house and invited to his table. The wife of the Mayor of Kingston, at the time of Mr. Bigelow's visit, and the wife of the Receiver-General, were of African descent; one of the most distinguished barristers on the island was a colored man, educated at an English university. At the Surrey Assize, where Sir Joshua Rowe presided, two colored lawyers were sitting at the barristers' table, and of the jury, all but three were colored. All the officers of the court, except the clerk, were colored. Seven tenths of the whole police force of the island, amounting to about 800 men, were estimated to be colored. In the Legislative Assembly, composed of from forty-eight to fifty members, ten or a dozen were colored. The public printers of the Legislature, who were also editors of the leading government paper, were both colored men. One or two black regiments were constantly kept under pay; and it is the evident policy of the government to place the local management of the island, as far as possible, under the control of people of color, while it is very likely, ultimately, to be surrendered entirely into their hands.

The colored people of the island seem to appreciate, in important respects, the advantages which freedom gives. A freehold of five acres will supply nearly all a negro's physical wants, and will also give him the privilege of voting. There are now over 100,000 belonging to the class of land proprietors, and the number is constantly increasing. The average property of each proprietor is estimated at about three acres. This number of landholders must be regarded as a very large one, when it is remembered that only seventeen years have passed since nearly all of them were slaves. The present tendency of things is for the island to pass into the hands of the blacks. What its future destiny may be, whether it will continue a colonial dependency of Great Britain, or have a separate government of its own, or be finally absorbed into the United States, is a question upon which we will not venture any prophetical speculations.

The principal obstacles to emigration arise out of difficulties which small capitalists may have to encounter in the purchase of land. A large part of the present proprietors reside abroad. This fact, and the different ways in which estates are involved, may, in many cases, lengthen out and embarrass negotiations between them and those who would be purchasers. There is also an indisposition to sell the large estates in fragments and parcels, while many of the planters discourage all sales of land to the blacks, from the fear that, by increasing their independence, it will raise the price of labor. Both of these obstacles, however, are merely temporary. The former must give way before the steady depreciation and impoverishment of estates as now managed, and the second must yield to more just views of the real interests of the island. In addition to other considerations which tend to make these difficulties less troublesome, it is well understood that the British government is ready to favor the immigration of colored people from the United States. It is desirous of vindicating the policy of emancipation. In doing this, it endeavors now to promote the interests of the colored population which is already there, and will welcome, in such ways as it can, those blacks from the United States, who, by their industry or intelligence, are likely to advance the prosperity of the island.

We have given, from Mr. Bigelow's work, this extended abstract of facts which bear on the subject of colonization in Jamaica, from the conviction that it would be useful to have them more generally known. For more particular information, we refer our readers to the book itself, as one which will abundantly repay perusal.

Of course, we do not commend colonization either in Jamaica or Africa as a panacea for all the evils of slavery, nor do we anticipate that colored colonies, outranking all others in wisdom and virtue, will suddenly become embodied Utopias. We have no intention of maintaining extravagancies of this sort. It is not necessary that colonization should be a full and complete antidote to slavery to make it worthy of consideration. Our object has been simply to show, that in the present state of the world, it furnishes an opportunity to the free black for a decided improvement of his own condition, and, still more, that of his children, and that well-arranged schemes of colonization would form a most useful part in any wise plan for the abolition of slavery. If it be competent to no more than this, it deserves the attention of every humane and every patriotic man.

In treating of what relates to the welfare of our black population, it is impossible to pass wholly by some of those questions of the day which owe their origin to slavery, and which, at certain points, are closely connected with the interests of the slave. If it were in accordance with the design of this article, it might give us the same pleasure that it does others, to discuss more fully, and under their more general aspects, these questions. But this would be aside from our present purpose; and in order not to be misunderstood, and not to embarrass the subject to which we shall confine ourselves with what is comparatively irrelevant, we would say explicitly, that in our remarks, we make no reference whatsoever to any recent legislation of Congress, in the way of expressing a judgment on its merits. Indeed, the views which we wish to present are not only quite independent of this legislation, regarded as wise or unwise, but they relate exclusively to great principles which underlie our organization as a people; — principles which are monopolized by no party, which ought not to be surrendered to party uses, and which are consistent with, and may be held by, those who entertain the most diverse opinions respecting particular measures of public policy. No matter what the duty of the whites may be in respect to the future, the great question with the blacks is, not what might have been, nor indeed what may hereafter be, but what are now the actual facts of their condition. Whatever their merits, whether such as we should have preferred, or such as we should not have preferred, — certain measures which bear on the condition of the blacks have become a part of the law of the land. The Constitution and the Union remain unbroken; the laws to which we have referred not only exist, but as a matter of fact — wrought, as they are, into the general framework and system of government — we suppose there can be little reason for any expectation that they will not continue to exist; the blacks live under them, and will continue to live under them; and in the mean while, it is a matter of much practical moment to them, that their true relations to the institutions of the country should be understood aright. In the discussions which have vexed the land, attention has been directed almost exclusively to the interests and duties of the whites. We wish, in regard to two principal points, to call attention to what, under the existing state of things, is for the interest of the blacks.

Foremost among the questions of the day is that which relates to the preservation of the Union. Of its importance to the general welfare, North and South, so far as the whites are concerned, there never has been a question, except among those who have had other objects in view than the prosperity of the whole country. There has doubtless been much diversity of opinion respecting the bearing of particular measures on the perpetuity of our institutions; and the long enjoyment of domestic peace may have made us comparatively insensible to its value, and to the conditions through which alone it can be preserved. There are those, too, who, in a blind devotion to some single end or interest, are ready to sacrifice all rights and interests, unless they can attain the single object at which they aim. But it is an instructive fact that, with these exceptions, of all those men who have most adorned our history, and who, by common consent, have been placed in the first rank as men of clear, far-seeing wisdom, however much they may have differed on other points, there is not one who has not regarded the preservation of the Union as the absolute and fundamental condition, not only of our general welfare as a people, but of preserving the most important rights which our institutions now secure to us. Nor do we suppose that the most emphatic words of Washington, and the most impassioned declarations and earnest warnings of the wisest men since his time, go beyond the calmest truth. It is difficult to see what could be gained by disunion in regard to any interest or any right, but quite easy to foresee the certainty of immeasurable loss. It would be like breaking up a noble ship, which, whatever its imperfections, still bears those on board safely across the seas, in order that the dismembered and scattered crew might find greater safety and independence on the loose rafts constructed out of the fragments. After the Revolution, Lord Sheffield, sharing in the belief which prevailed in England of the impracticability of any permanent and peaceful confederacy among us, prophesied, that from the necessary results of disunion, this country must be comparatively powerless; and confidently declared that England had as little reason "to deprecate the resolves of the German Diet as of the American Congress." And except for that Union, which, as we look back on the difficulties in the way of its formation, seems now to have been the work of Providence rather than of man, these evil auguries would have fallen far short of the reality. So absolutely essential is the Union to the maintenance and progressive diffusion of all the interests and rights which we most value, that the recent agitation of the subject will have been one of the fortunate events in our history, if it leave behind a more general and vivid conviction of the necessity of abiding by that Constitution which makes us a nation.

But while all this is universally assented to, there are those who seem to think that a dissolution of the Union would, in some undefined and inexplicable way, redound to the advantage of the blacks. We do not understand on what such an expectation can be founded. So far from it, of the 23,000,000 of people within our borders, there are none to whom the Union is more important, none to whom disunion would be more instantly and hopelessly disastrous, than the slave population at the South. Hard as the fate of the negro now is, it would then be hopeless. Were the Union dissolved, the immediate consequence would be, that, at the South, all thought of the abolition of slavery, except through insurrection, would be at an end. Were the slaves emancipated, they must still remain where they are; for the resources of the South would be insufficient to remove them, while the northern States, some of which even now refuse to admit free blacks within their limits, would lend no aid. In large districts of country, the liberated slaves would outnumber the whites. Color, race, the traditional sentiments and customs on both sides, would keep them apart, and create a feeling of jealous antagonism. The inevitable results of such a state would be deplorable enough; a probable result would be the gradual deterioration, as in Mexico and South America, of both blacks and whites: while a not improbable one would be a war of races, followed by extermination, or expulsion from the soil, or the enslavement of the weaker by the stronger party; — and calamitous as this must be to all, the blacks could hardly fail to be the chief victims. With such prospects before them, those southern men who now look forward to emancipation as a kind of millennium, would, in case of disunion, become the strenuous supporters of slavery. For the protection of the whites, and to prevent the escape of slaves, the slave laws would become more rigorous. The free blacks would be looked upon with ever-increasing distrust, and liberty to them would cease to be a boon. All the interests of the South, like a ship wedged inextricably in one of the drifting floes of Arctic ice, would be inseparably bound in with slavery. In this struggle of life and death, the fears of the white, far more than the law can do, would prevent his giving the black any instruction which tended to develop his rational powers. Slavery demands space, and nothing would hinder the South from extending the territory of slavery further into Mexico, or from annexing to its narrowed empire the island of Cuba. Those many helps and restraints which arise out of the connection of North and South, and which accrue to the advantage of the slave, would be gone, and the two races, with all their implacable jealousies, would be enclosed together in an arena from which escape would be hopeless.

Of the importance to the whole country, that whatever is done for the benefit of the blacks should be done in subjection to the Constitution, it would seem mere trifling even to speak. But while, for the sake of the general good, the necessity, in all such efforts, of proceeding by constitutional methods is recognized, it is not so much considered that the welfare of none is more immediately dependent on maintaining the steady sovereignty of law, than that of the slave. Any violation of law, though intended for his benefit, must finally result in nothing but mischief to his class. If, through the action of inconsiderate friends, the blacks are brought into a position of antagonism to law, they must inevitably be the victims. So universal and reasonable is the conviction, that the rights and welfare of all are identified with the maintenance of law while it is law, and until it is changed by constitutional methods, that any settled purpose of resisting the law would alienate from the blacks whatever sympathy is now felt for them, and cause them to be regarded as the dangerous enemies of social order. Instead of being looked on as sufferers under hard and unequal institutions, they would be regarded as the foes of the public peace; and what their fate must be in such a conflict, it requires no prophet to foresee. The strong may sometimes safely defy the law, but the weak find their best protection in law, even though it be imperfect; while their best hope is, by preserving the sympathy of the humane and just, to secure its gradual improvement.

There is much, doubtless, to deplore in our national spirit and in our institutions, so far as they bear on the condition of the black. But we will not close this article with words of evil omen. Nor is it needed. To us, the history of the last two years is, on the whole, an encouraging one. The country has passed through a crisis which has tried its institutions from corner to keystone. Questions of absolutely vital moment have been raised and fiercely discussed. In looking back on the aspect of public affairs at the beginning of 1850, and comparing it with what now appears, who is there but must acknowledge that we have reasons for the profoundest gratitude? The existence of the Union seemed then to be at stake. The conquests which war had gained from a foreign power, threatened to involve the land in the worst evils of domestic strife; while slavery seemed ready, by a sudden and vast enlargement of its area, to fix itself immovably on this continent. It is necessary to remember the fears of that period, in order to appreciate what we now enjoy. The boldest and most sanguine friends of free institutions then did not dare to hope, what now has become reality. The whole of the immense territory, extorted from Mexico, so far as its condition had not been determined by previous legislation, appears, practically, to have ranged itself on the side of freedom; while almost the sole qualification on this vast expansion of free territory, has been what was in substance the re-enactment, for the recovery of fugitive slaves, of a law which, in its essential characteristics, had been in existence for half a century. We are very far from saying that all has happened as we should have chosen, had choice been within our power; but this is no reason why, in summing up the results of two years of agitation respecting subjects involved in the greatest difficulties, we should be blind to the good and sensitive only to the evil. And when we consider the conflicting parties banded against each other, and the complications of so many States with antagonistic interests, we cannot but think that the issue of the crisis has, *on the whole*, been such as ought to gratify every man who believes in the worth of the Union or in the value of free institutions. Within the whole period since the adoption of the Constitution and the abolition of slavery in the Northern States, free institutions have never made more progress, never done more to gain a commanding place and an assurance of final triumph, than during the last two years.

There is, also, to our minds, in the character of the struggle which has agitated the country, much that gives encouragement for the future. When the time comes for opposing parties among us at the North to do each other justice, we think the fact will be recognized, that on both sides, principles of fundamental importance have been maintained.

There are two sentiments absolutely essential to the healthy existence of a republic; — that of a vigilant sensibility to personal rights, and that of loyalty to law. Free institutions grow out of a prevailing sense of the value and sacredness of personal rights. We need to have fostered among us a perpetual watchfulness in regard to the rights of the individual, and a jealousy of all encroachment upon them. On the other hand, without loyalty to law, which is the guardian of all the rights of all, and the protection of the weak against the strong, we are remanded back to a barbarism in which the individual loses all those personal rights which he cannot maintain with his own hand. These two sentiments are to each other as body and soul, which cannot exist on earth except united. A sensitive regard to personal rights without loyalty to law, would turn a republic into an anarchy; and reverence for law, unbalanced by this regard for the freedom and rights of the individual, would become a mere tame, obsequious submission to the chance despotism of the hour. A state of things bringing into conflict these two sentiments, which ought to have been blended in indissoluble union, has given their most important characteristics to the party divisions of the time. At the North, it has not been a question of money, or power, or prosperity, but of principles which lie at the foundation of society. It is not wonderful that they should have taken deep hold of the passions of a people accustomed, on all subjects, to think and act with a persistent and serious earnestness; nor is it surprising that, sundered, exaggerated, put into violent opposition, their adherents should have been mutually repelled into extremes which none of them would soberly approve.

Great, however, as has been the temporary mischief, we cannot regard it as all evil. It has aroused the nation to consider the relations which liberty, law, and union sustain to each other. Nay, we derive encouragement for the future, from the very violence of the contest. Its history shows that, at the least, we possess that which is a chief condition of force and energy in men and nations, — a capacity for strong moral convictions. This party strife has had some of the characteristics of a religious war. On one side, men have believed that they were doing God service by defending at all hazards what they deemed the personal rights of the slave; and on the other side, they have equally believed they were serving God in defending the sanctity of law, and in so doing, defending in the best way, and to the greatest extent, the rights of both slave and free. There have been the bitterness and intolerance of a conscientious purpose on both sides. Calmness and mutual justice have been wanting. Especially there have been wanting clear and discriminating ideas respecting the relations of the individual to society, in regard to the point at which the rights of one must give way to the rights of all; or in other words, of the point where personal freedom must yield to the law, through which alone the freedom of all has any permanent protection. Much is to be regretted; passion, injustice, intolerance are to be regretted; but not that personal rights are held sacred, nor that law is honored. Instead of alarming us, whatever indicates the existence of such feelings is a trustworthy symptom of the healthful state of the public mind. We hardly know which we should most dread, — insensibility to the worth of individual freedom, or insensibility to the importance of maintaining law. In either case, free institutions would be at an end, and society relapse into barbarism, or sink into that worse than savage state which follows a worn out civilization. But where men — who are not more individuals than social beings — seek freedom in union, and through that union which exists by means of law, and where those sentiments prevail which make freedom, thus sought and limited, sacred, there is still youthful blood circulating through the social body; and if it be sometimes attended with the diseases of youth, it brings with it also vigor, and elasticity, and hope.

www.ingramcontent.com/pod-product-compliance
Lightning Source LLC
LaVergne TN
LVHW011123110826
845150LV00008B/2231

* 9 7 8 1 4 1 8 1 9 5 2 3 6 *